Original title:
The Meaning of Life (and Where I Left It)

Copyright © 2025 Creative Arts Management OÜ
All rights reserved.

Author: Sophia Kingsley
ISBN HARDBACK: 978-1-80566-249-5
ISBN PAPERBACK: 978-1-80566-544-1

The Quest for Purpose

I searched for my socks, but found a shoe,
A quest for reason turned into a zoo.
The more I ponder, the less I see,
Maybe purpose is just having tea.

I asked the cat, she just licked her paw,
Said life's a puzzle without a law.
I tried to fit pieces, but they wouldn't align,
Perhaps I'll just nap, and call it divine.

Chasing Fleeting Moments

I chased a butterfly, it flew away,
Moments are like sweets that spoil in a day.
I waved at a rainbow, it blinked and then
Vanished like my lunch, my hopes gone again.

I tried to catch laughter, it slipped from my grip,
A giggle, a snort, all lost on the trip.
So I scatter my joy like confetti in air,
And hope someone finds it, with room to spare.

Footprints on a Fading Path

I walked on a path of bright golden leaves,
But left all my snacks where the chipmunk heaves.
Tracking my steps as I craved a good bite,
Life's like a stroll with a snack just out of sight.

With footprints that vanish under the sun,
I pondered the race, is it ever really fun?
But life's like my garden, it grows wild with cheer,
As long as I keep losing, I'll persevere.

Threads of Intention

I knit with intentions made up of yarn,
But somehow my sweater looks more like a barn.
Each stitch is a hope, each row a new plot,
Yet here I am tangled, guessing my lot.

I wove dreams of grandeur, a tapestry bright,
But ended up draping myself in the night.
Maybe these threads are just there for a jest,
In life's grand design, I'm simply a guest.

Whispers of Existence

In a sock drawer, dreams reside,
Hiding from the laundry tide.
Coffee spills and laughter reigns,
Searching for lost silly brains.

Between the crumbs and old receipts,
Life's lesson? Laughter beats.
When in doubt, dance on floors,
Children should know where fun soars.

Ephemeral Journeys

Life's a bus ride, full of bumps,
Change your seat or risk the lumps.
With snacks in hand and smiles bright,
We'll figure out this silly plight.

Maps are for those who fear the wrong,
But going astray can feel so strong.
Lost in fun, we've found our way,
Who knew confusion led to play?

Fragments of the Soul

A puzzle piece under the chair,
Yelling, "Put me in with flair!"
Life's a game of hide-and-seek,
Silly giggles, nothing bleak.

Colors clash on every wall,
Decor dreams? They're now a brawl.
In existential crises, I muse,
Is it time for more ice cream to choose?

Echoes in the Void

Whispers dance in empty halls,
Chasing echoes, making calls.
Your best sock is hiding here,
While jokes linger, loud and clear.

The calendar's filled with crossed-out plans,
Yet here I am, laughing with fans.
Finding purpose in coffee spills,
And in those naps, we chase the thrills.

The Heartbeat of Forgotten Places

In a garden where socks tend to roam,
I found a lost key that unlocked my home.
Cats hold council beneath the old tree,
They laughed at my shoes, 'Who wears two left feet?'

A toaster once told me it dreams of the sea,
While my coffee pot whispers, 'What about me?'
I asked a lost bird where it thought of flight,
It said, 'I'll just follow the crumbs of delight.'

Seeking a Home Among the Stars

I packed my bags with some cosmic dust,
And left my socks, though I had to adjust.
A space cat meowed, suggesting a trip,
To find a nice planet for my coffee sip.

A star winked at me, 'Why so serious, friend?'
The moon laughed and said, 'This is just pretend!'
With a twinkle of eyes and my shimmering grin,
I danced on a comet, where the fun would begin.

Tracing the Patterns of Existence

I drew my life's path with crayons and glue,
But the dog stole my paper; now what can I do?
A wise old shoe said, 'Just follow your heart,'
But it led me to puddles; that's not where I'd start.

I traced all the lines that life often bends,
Found a lost penny; it called me 'my friend.'
With a wink and a smile, we decided to roam,
A quest for the best nachos to call our home.

The Prints of Time on My Soul

Time left a mark, like a chocolate stain,
On my favorite shirt, oh the joys of the mundane!
I tried to wash it but it laughed with glee,
'You can't scrub away the fun that is me!'

I wandered through memories, all jumbled and strange,
Where laughter and chaos do happily range.
Each print is a story, a giggle, a sigh,
In the scrapbook of life, under a wild sky.

The Journey Beyond the Horizon

I packed my bags, set out for gold,
But I tripped on a sock, so bold.
My map was upside down, you see,
Now I'm lost on a giant flea.

A parrot squawked, "You missed the turn!"
I said, "That's fine, I love to learn!"
We danced on waves made of jelly,
Turns out I'm quite the silly fella.

Oh, the stars wink down a bright path,
But I fell in a puddle, oh what a laugh!
With every misstep, I find delight,
Sometimes lost is where I feel right.

So here I journey without a care,
Each wrong turn adds flavor to the air.
Forget the prize at the end of strife,
I find my joy in this crazy life.

Threads of Serendipity

I dropped my sandwich on the floor,
It landed right at destiny's door.
A cat played fetch with my old hat,
Now it's famous, how about that?

A bus went by, with wheels of cheese,
I jumped aboard, oh, who'd want to tease?
We cruised through towns on stilts so high,
The sky was pink, I swear, oh my!

I tripped on fate, fell into a pie,
The baker laughed, I don't know why.
With every laugh, a lesson spins,
Life's tapestry, where chaos wins.

So here's to mishaps, small and grand,
Every detour, each grain of sand.
In this wild weave where I linger,
Serendipity dances on my finger.

In the Heart of Uncertainty

I woke up late, my clock went nuts,
My hair looked like it met some guts.
With coffee spilled all down my shirt,
I pondered if this is just dessert.

The cat is plotting, I swear it's true,
While I'm debating what to do.
Should I nap or should I bake?
Life's all questions—none I make!

A squirrel stole my sandwich quick,
I chased it down, that little trick!
He chattered loud, I swore I heard,
"Life's a riddle, that's the word!"

But through the haze of doubts profound,
Amid the nuts and laughter found,
I dance with whimsy, take a chance,
In the heart of chaos, I find my dance.

When Questions Become Companions

Where's my sock? It must know,
Why do birds never wear shoes?
Is the fridge a portal to realms?
Maybe it simply likes to snooze.

Every morning, I ask my mug,
Is coffee just dreams in disguise?
What if my cat is the wise one?
Her purring holds all the good vibes.

I question the moon, why so bright?
Does it ever get tired, you think?
Or is it just high on its glow?
Riding the stars, having a drink?

Life's quirks are like playful kids,
They giggle and dart all around.
In chaos, questions run rampant,
Hiding where clarity's found.

Beneath the Surface of Silence

In a quiet room full of noise,
The walls hold secrets, lost and found.
The chair whispers tales of the past,
While the table giggles without sound.

The clock chimes with a snicker of time,
It tips its hat, but never stays.
Did the dust gather thoughts of its own?
Or just plot a dance, in lazy ways?

In silence, I hear a faint laugh,
The curtains play peek-a-boo, it seems.
Who knew solitude had a sense,
Of humor wrapped up in sweet dreams?

Between breaths, life stumbles and trips,
Like a toddler learning to run.
Maybe silence is just a prank,
A jester hanging out in the sun.

Embracing the Unknown

What lurks beyond my comfy bed?
A world where socks seem to appear.
Do they party while I'm asleep?
Inviting my shoes for some cheer?

Maps are decent, though they may lie,
Leading to places that just don't exist.
Perhaps it's best, just going with it,
Life's plot twists, a comic book twist.

I ask my mirror, what do you see?
Does it snicker back or hold its grin?
Each day's an adventure designed for laughs,
With surprises and mishaps to spin.

To embrace the unknown, like a dance,
With two left feet tripping along,
Life's oddities chant a sweet tune,
Reminding us where we belong.

The Art of Letting Go

Holding onto worries like glue,
They weigh me down, a heavy pack.
What if I dropped them all right now?
And floated out like a quirky flak?

Each grudge is a pet I can't feed,
They nibble at joy, consume my days.
Releasing them like balloons in spring,
Letting the wind choose our own ways.

Fears clutter thoughts, like old junk mail,
Why hoard the what-ifs in my mind?
Each toss brings freedom, and I feel light,
Laughter awaits just beyond the blind.

Life's a circus, let go of the ring,
Don't juggle the past with a frown.
Trust the chaos, dance on the edge,
And wear a smile, not a crown.

Whispers of Beneath the Surface

In a world of ducks and shoes,
I ponder on what I might lose.
Will I find my missing socks?
Or just the odd, forgotten clocks?

The cat sits on the quiet chair,
Judging me with her cool stare.
Was it once my life I tossed?
Or just a sandwich I embossed?

Searching for crumbs, I delve deep,
Among old toys and dirt heaps.
I swear that life's just a big joke,
Like trying to learn the rhythm of folk.

Among the layers, secrets hide,
Like that time I tried to take a ride.
I laughed, I cried, and then I slipped,
My hotdog dreams about to be flipped.

Signposts in a Crowded Mind

Lost my keys and found old maps,
Faded trails and cricket claps.
Where's the route to joy, you say?
It's down the hall, or far away.

I ask the parrot for some hints,
It squawks back, as my patience slints.
Maybe life's a scavenger hunt,
With ice cream cones as the main stunt.

A yellow sign says 'Turn Here!'
But I went left and drank some beer.
Maps are scribbles, thoughts like wind,
I'll smile and wave, I'm still your friend.

My thoughts feel like a wiggly worm,
A twisty path with no set term.
Yet here I dance and laugh aloud,
Chasing rainbows, lost in the crowd.

The Rhythms of an Unwritten Day

Sunrise brings the coffee grind,
Fluffy clouds and thoughts entwined.
What's this dance of socks and shoes?
A morning shuffle with local news.

The clock ticks on a crazy beat,
As I step on crumbs beneath my feet.
Life's a song sung off-key,
With jazz hands flailing goofily.

Doodles swirl upon my page,
In a circus of everyday rage.
Chasing balloons in endless flight,
Under a sky that's somewhat bright.

I trip on laughter, fall on grace,
Embrace the chaos of this place.
With every misstep, I find my way,
On this unwritten, silly day.

Where Echoes Find Their Voice

In the canyon of my thoughts so loud,
Echos mumble, drawing a crowd.
'Hello!' they call, as I politely grin,
Wondering where the logic's been.

A squirrel taps her tiny toes,
In rhythm with my coffee woes.
Life's a riddle, maybe a quilt,
With pieces sewn from laughter built.

Whispers here blend with chaotic song,
Is that a right note or just plain wrong?
Each bounce of sound brings a clue,
Maybe it's just my old shoe.

I giggle at the echoes near,
Twirling 'round without a care.
Where is my voice in this great din?
Oh, right! It's hiding! Let's try again!

Beneath the Veil of Existence

I searched for wisdom, found a shoe,
A single sock and a rolling pin too.
Who knew enlightenment could be so neat,
With random objects scattered at my feet.

A talking cat strolled by on the street,
Claiming it knows the tricks to defeat.
I asked for advice but just got a purr,
The meaning eludes me, oh cosmic blur.

Lost in the Tapestry of Time

I wandered through the days like a clumsy fly,
Stuck on the wall or perhaps in a pie.
Time's a wizard with a sense of humor,
It juggles the past like a frantic tumor.

Now clocks tick loud, they scream at me,
As if I'm the one who's lost the key.
I step on the gas, yet enjoy the ride,
Life is a party where socks are mismatched wide.

Shadows of Tomorrow

Tomorrow's shadow dances on my wall,
Wearing mismatched shoes, having a ball.
It whispers secrets in a silly tone,
As if my couch is made of pure goldstone.

I chase after wisdom like a flat tire,
Rolling aimlessly, with dreams caught in fire.
Yet laughter ensues with every spill,
Life's wobbly journey is a comic thrill.

Reflections in a Broken Mirror

I gazed in shards to see my face,
A jigsaw puzzle with a comedic grace.
Each jagged piece tells a silly tale,
Of a life where sanity seemed to pale.

But in those cracks, I found delight,
A rainbow of chaos striking just right.
I'll wear my laughter like a cap and gown,
In this peculiar circus, I'll never frown.

Echoes of Yesterday

I searched for wisdom in my sock,
A sage who whispered, 'Just wear a clock!'
The cat gave me a knowing glance,
While I danced with fate, lost in a trance.

Old books piled high, tools of my trade,
Maps to my dreams all faded away.
Yet, in the chaos, I found a cheer,
Life's silly strolls are worth the jeer.

Each coffee spill, a lesson pure,
Like love notes scribbled, a wild allure.
Laughter's the compass, never a bore,
In the end, it's just a fun little tour.

With crumbs of joy and giggles that bend,
I've stitched my tapestry, thread by friend.
So here's to the echoes, the laughs we build,\nEmbrace the absurd, let joy be distilled.

The Heart's Compendium

My heart's a library, shelves full of dreams,
But misfiled entries fall into seams.
Where's that book on how to floss?
It vanished, like my last find that was boss!

Romantic comedies, each page a jest,
Love's awkward moments, we never protest.
A pile of socks, mismatched but bold,
Reflects the adventures that never grow old.

A guide for the curious, a laugh every week,
Turn the page, find joy in the meek.
In chapters of mishaps, the plot thickens fast,
Every blunder I make will forever last.

So, open the cover, dive into the spree,
Life's farcical tales, just let them be.
The heart knows the rhythm, absurd and divine,
With a wink and a chuckle, we'll sip on the wine.

Navigate the Unseen

Life's a map, but why is it blank?
With directions lost, I drive to a prank.
At every turn, the GPS fails,
Yet laughter guides me through the gales.

Just yesterday, I slipped on a charm,
A moment of grace? Nah, just alarm.
The path's filled with glitter, a treasure untold,
In each silly stumble, our stories unfold.

We take the wrong train, end up in Greece,
Ordering pizza and shouting for peace.
My compass spins, with every good laugh,
Navigating chaos, that's my new path.

So here's to the journeys, the wrongs made right,
With maps drawn in crayon, life's sheer delight.
Embrace the unseen, let laughter abound,
In circuits of joy, may our hearts be found.

Beneath the Surface

Scooting through life on a banana peel,
I ponder deep thoughts with a side of oatmeal.
Why's the grass greener, what's fueling the dream?
A rubber duck told me, 'It's all a meme!'

The surface is shiny, but what's underneath?
A stash of old jokes, and last week's wreath.
I found a tin can, it whispered my fears,
Turned out it was just a drawer of tears.

Cracks in the pavement hold secrets galore,
Like absurd little tales, we giggle and snore.
Underneath it all, the mess is divine,
With friends and some humor, the stars truly shine.

So let's lift the rug, reveal the delight,
Dance with the shadows, embrace silly fright.
With laughter as currency, we'll thrive and we'll live,
In the treasure of chaos, there's joy to give.

Lost in the Echo of a Dream

I searched for wisdom in the mall,
Only found my hat and a pack of gum.
A voice said, 'Life's a free-for-all!'
I asked, 'But where's the fun?'

In existential aisles I wandered long,
Thoughts like shopping carts, full and wild.
I laughed out loud, it felt so wrong,
Like being lost as a toddler-child.

A cosmic joke, or was it fate?
The clock struck three at quarter past.
I thought I'd ponder while I wait,
But ended up late, not unsurpassed.

So here I stand in my own play,
Life's a sitcom, rehearsed just right.
With laughter, snacks, and games to play,
I'll find my path, or at least tonight.

The Geometry of Existence

I drew a triangle, thought it deep,
With angles sharp like my sense of style.
In circles spun, I lost some sleep,
Pondering life's odd, quirky aisle.

Definition's tricky; let's make it fun,
A square sometimes fits a round hole too.
I laughed with pi, we opted to run,
Between lines, curves, and a joyful crew.

The radius stretched, my heart took flight,
I danced among proofs in a wobbly way.
In this math of moments, both wrong and right,
I claimed that joy is what I'd convey.

So grab a ruler, let's measure cheer,
In the classroom of life, we gather round.
With laughs and shapes that disappear,
We'll figure it out, then hit the ground.

Fragments of a Wayward Soul

I tried to catch my falling thoughts,
But they slipped like buttered toast.
Each crumb a fragment, lessons taught,
I giggled at my brain's strange ghost.

I wandered paths of fancy dreams,
Where socks remained in hiding places.
With silly grins and playful schemes,
I chased reflections, shared our faces.

Lost keys jangled with a melody,
Each note a sign from the cosmos bright.
"Just be absurd!" they sang with glee,
Embrace the chaos, forget the fight.

In every puzzle, pieces stray,
A puzzle made for laughs, it seems.
Each little version shows the way,
With humor woven through our dreams.

An Odyssey of Little Things

I set sail on a paper boat,
With crumpled plans and a silly grin.
Every wave, a joke I wrote,
As giggles danced with the wind's spin.

The stars above winked, oh so bright,
While clouds provided comic relief.
Each raindrop fell like a punchline right,
In a sketchbook filled with belief.

Between the waves, snacks were found,
And hiccups led to laughter loud.
The tides carried whispers all around,
Of tiny moments that made me proud.

So here's to life and its little things,
To silly songs and afterthoughts.
With every breeze, a new joy springs,
In this odyssey of happy knots.

As the Sun Sets on Certainty

Every answer I seek seems to run,
Like a cat with a laser, just having fun.
I chase in a frenzy, I trip on a dream,
Reality hangs by a thread and a scream.

Sipping my coffee, I ponder the stew,
Of questions that lead me to who knows where too.
With socks on my feet, mismatched and bizarre,
I giggle at truths that are so very far.

Cracking a joke with the wise old sage,
His laughter is louder than my next stage.
I fumble through life, a smile on my skin,
For I know I'm a mess, yet I still want to win.

As twilight unfolds, my worries subside,
I dance with my dog; he's my ultimate guide.
In the waltz of the night, we twirl and we spin,
Finding joy in the chaos, that's where we begin.

The Garden of Unanswered Prayers

In a garden so lush, with weeds as my cloak,
I tend to my wishes, I giggle and choke.
Each rose has a thorn, as sharp as my wit,
Planting dreams in the soil, I shovel some grit.

The daisies are gossiping over lost socks,
While lilacs discuss the next TikTok stocks.
In this patch of confusion, a sunflower beams,
Reminding me daily to water my dreams.

Beetles debate what it means to be grand,
While ants hold a meeting to form a rock band.
I grin at the madness, this chaos so bright,
In this tangled-up garden, my heart feels the light.

With butterflies flitting, the clouds race the breeze,
I find shade in laughter, with giggles to seize.
For though some things wilt, and others take flight,
I cherish this garden, my humorous sight.

Journeying Through the Unfathomable

With a map made of crayon, I venture afar,
Searching for wisdom… or maybe a bar.
Through mountains of laundry and valleys of strife,
I stumble on questions that sharpen my knife.

The compass spins wildly, directions unclear,
While I trip on my shoelace and tumble in beer.
Each step is an auction of moments I trod,
With laughter as currency, I barter with God.

Lost in the labyrinth of my own crazy mind,
I wave to the shadows, so quirky and blind.
For the path's an adventure, even if strange,
And I'm learning to laugh at each twist and each change.

Through the whirlpool of nonsense, I leap with a cheer,
Every hiccup a lesson, each giggle sincere.
In this journey of wild, I find a strange peace,
For the riddles of life seem to never quite cease.

Maps Made of Memories

I pull out my map, it's a jumbled-up mess,
With heart-shaped trails and a whimsical guess.
From birthday balloons to that time I got lost,
Each place tells a story; oh, what a cost!

The X marks the spot where I danced with my cat,
And a fork in the road where I first ate a hat.
With laughter and love scribbled all o'er the page,
I plot out my journeys, an adventurous stage.

A bridge made of laughter spans rivers of tears,
While I scribble my dreams as I dodge all my fears.
Each line is a tale, each squiggle a pause,
For the journey is wacky, and I'm just finding cause.

Through the valleys of time, I sail with a grin,
In this map of my life, every turn is a win.
So here's to the stories, my memories' gleam,
For the roads get much brighter when traveled with gleam.

Unraveled Threads

In a sweater tangled tight,
I sought the warmth of light.
Each stitch a puzzle spun,
Making sense of all the fun.

The cat jumped in my lap,
Thinking it's a cozy trap.
I chase my thoughts like mice,
Climbing chaos, oh so nice!

Yarn balls roll, they dance,
Every knot a silly chance.
With laughter weaving through,
Life's a craft, where all is new.

So let the colors blend,
In this absurd little trend.
As I stitch my tale tonight,
I find joy in the slight and bright.

Clarity in Chaos

Amidst the clutter and the din,
I search for wisdom, where to begin?
Laundry piles and dishes stacked,
Not one thought is ever tracked.

A sock flies by, it makes me grin,
Maybe I'll wear it as my pin.
With coffee spills and crumbs galore,
I sip and laugh – can't ask for more!

The world spins fast, like a Disney ride,
I scream and whirl, with arms spread wide.
In chaos, laughter is my guide,
Finding order when I confide.

So here's to life's wild and crazy plan,
With giggles stitched in every span.
In all this mess, I dare to thrive,
Happy chaos keeps us alive!

Lighthouses of Purpose

Tiny beams in foggy nights,
Guide me through with their bright lights.
I stumble over ancient rocks,
Laughing at my mismatched socks.

Does a lighthouse see my plight?
"Yo!" I shout, "Please guide my flight!"
Yet each wave just splashes back,
A comical, uncharted track.

I dream of sailing distant seas,
But can't find my other keys.
A compass spins like my mind,
In these waters, joy I find.

I may not know where I'll belong,
But with a wink, I'll sing my song.
These lighthouses, they laugh and glow,
Pointing to places I can go!

Forgotten Footprints

In the sand, I left a mark,
But the tide rolled in, a playful lark.
Each wave a twist in my grand tale,
Washing away my forgotten trail.

I danced under the sunlit sky,
Where footprints laugh and memories fly.
"Hey there, waves, come dance with me!"
They splash back joy, wild and free.

Oh, to remember what was lost,
The tiny moments, what a cost!
But who needs a path to follow?
When giggles bounce, they surely swallow.

So here I stand, on shifting ground,
In every step, new joys unbound.
Each footprint gone? Not really true,
I dance in the chaos, one adieu!

Exploring the Edges of Reality

In a land where socks go to hide,
I ponder the truths of the great wide.
Are we just players in a cosmic game?
Or is it all just the universe's shame?

With every step, I trip on a thought,
Is this all tangled? Or simply distraught?
The cat stares deep, judging my quest,
Perhaps it's just these chips I digest.

I dance with shadows, a tango of fate,
Finding laughter in the oddest of state.
Do pigeons conspire while I take a seat?
And discuss the secrets of crumbs at my feet?

Reality bends, like a spoon in my hand,
These cosmic mysteries I hardly withstand.
Yet with a giggle and a wink of the eye,
I embrace the absurd as I ponder and fly.

The Puzzle of My Unseen Self

I search for the pieces that seem to be lost,
In mirrors that show me a heavily cost.
Am I the sum of all my bad days?
Or just a lost sock in life's twisted maze?

Questions like jigsaw puzzles take flight,
Each answer unraveled is stitched with delight.
I ask my reflection, a partner in crime,
"Hey there, is living a form of a mime?"

The echoes of chaos laugh in the dark,
As I trip over meanings like a bull in a park.
Who knew life's lesson would sprout from a crease?
Or from where my sandwich fell in a piece?

So I toast to the quirks in this jumbled riddle,
Life's playful jests, a cosmic middle.
With every fumble, I find my own way,
Between the lost verses of yesterday's play.

Finding Light in Shadows

In the depths of dim corners, I stumble and twirl,
Chasing after echoes in a whimsy whirl.
Do shadows have secrets? Like hats on a bear?
Or wisdom so old, with dust in its hair?

I flick on the switch, but what do I see?
A dance of the silly, a light-hearted spree.
Perhaps the shadows are just trying to play,
In the bright hues of a half-moon's sway.

Unearthing the giggles where darkness has fled,
Like ketchup on fries, or a sandwich misread.
I laugh with the whispers that echo my thoughts,
In shadows we find what each laughter bought.

So I skip through the twilight, all giddy and spry,
Finding joy in the laughter that floats by.
For who knew a shadow could shine so divine,
When dancing with whimsy, a truth that's benign?

Notes from a Celestial Wanderer

I drift through the cosmos on pancakes of light,
With syrupy stars as companions of night.
Do Martians wear socks with holes at the seams?
Or do they prefer dreams topped with whipped creams?

Taken aback by the vastness so wild,
I scribble my thoughts as a cosmic child.
Gravity's play is a slapstick affair,
With planets like marbles rolling anywhere.

I collected some stardust, sprinkled with mischief,
As I barter with comets for a pop of festivity.
What's a shooting star without a belly laugh?
Or black holes that giggle at the space-time path?

Each note I pen is a cosmic delight,
In a universe sketchbook, my quirky flight.
So I wave to the planets gone by in a wink,
In this whimsical journey, I just smile and think.

Threads of Intention

In a world of twist and turns,
I lost my sock, and there it burns.
Each day I search, with laugh and cheer,
Life's missing pieces simply disappear.

A sandwich left on the kitchen shelf,
Reminds me of my hidden self.
With every bite, I find a clue,
Maybe mustard's what I was meant to do.

A line of thread, in colors bright,
I pull and tug with all my might.
But end results can come askew,
Like a bowtie made from old cat stew.

So here I dance, with mismatched shoes,
Spinning tales of all my blues.
For laughs and hiccups form the best part,
Of my quirky and loved-up heart.

In Pursuit of Wholeness

I woke up late, my coffee's cold,
Searching for wisdom, so I'm told.
My pants are inside out—what a sight!
Is this the clue to morning's light?

Chasing dreams in a cereal box,
I find lost treasures—not just old socks.
With every spoon, I ponder life,
Of cake, of pie, of laughter rife.

Perhaps it's hidden in my cat's purr,
Her wise insights make my thoughts stir.
But when I ask, she yawns and sleeps,
Guess there's no meaning, just naps and leaps.

On this quest, my compass spins,
In circles round, where laughter wins.
With jokes and jests, I take the ride,
Life's a game—enjoy the slide!

The Dance of Fate

Under the stars, I trip and fall,
Blaming the universe for it all.
Life's a waltz with two left feet,
Yet I twirl and leap to the offbeat.

A slice of pizza flies through the air,
It lands on my head—what a hair affair!
With toppings crowned, I'm feeling great,
Maybe this is my destined plate!

Each stumble brings laughter, that's my song,
In this circus, I find where I belong.
Dancing with spills and joyful grins,
With each wild turn, my soul wins.

So join me here, in this quirky fate,
Where mischief reigns and joy is great.
Let's dance through life without any care,
With pizza hats, who wouldn't dare?

Corners of Consciousness

In the kitchen, I find a clue,
A cookie jar calling, oh so true.
I ponder meaning with each bite,
Chocolate chips feel just right!

Peeking under the couch for fun,
What lies beneath? A dust bunny run.
It whispers secrets of lost dreams,
Or perhaps just leftover ice cream.

I looked inside my fridge today,
Found last week's pizza, in dismay.
Yet in that stale slice, I see gold,
In every laugh, a tale is told.

Exploring corners, with silly thoughts,
Where wisdom hides and laughter's sought.
Let's embrace this clueless strife,
Finding joy in the chaos of life.

A Journey to the Heart of Wonder

I packed my bags with socks and dreams,
Chasing joy while life just teems.
A map in hand, I lost my way,
Found a cat who stole my stay.

In the garden of unmade beds,
I asked the flowers where to head.
They just laughed and waved their stems,
A symphony of gentle gems.

With ice cream cones and silly hats,
I danced with gnomes and chatty chats.
Life's a riddle, light and spry,
Just don't ask me why, oh why!

So here I roam, a curious fool,
Seeking answers that break the rule.
In every stumble, every slide,
I find the joy I cannot hide.

Constellations of Questions

Stars above whisper sarcastic notes,
While I ponder why my sock floats.
Do ducks play chess when no one sees?
And do they care about worldly fees?

I scribble down my moonlit dreams,
In coffee cups and silly schemes.
The universe giggles, a shimmering tease,
As I ponder life under swaying trees.

Why do we blink in synchronized style?
Is evolution just life's own trial?
Each question floats like a feathered kite,
In the breeze of laughter, pure delight.

So let's toast to stars on this cosmic stage,
To questions that dance, our inner sage.
In the comedy of existence, we find our song,
In the void of wonder, where we all belong.

The Silence That Speaks Volumes

In stillness, I found my loudest cheer,
The fridge hums wisdom, oh so clear.
Behind closed doors, the echoes tease,
As my plants debate on sonic breeze.

I listen close to the clock's sly tick,
Each second a riddle, each minute a trick.
The silence shrugs, and snickers too,
Reminding me of things I thought I knew.

Do shadows plot when we're not around?
Competing for snacks we haven't found?
In the quiet, I giggle, neck deep in noise,
In laughter's absence, I find my joys.

So let the silence take a bow,
It's louder than any raucous wow.
In delightful whispers, we figure it out,
With silent jokes all about.

Wherever Dreams Might Lead

I built a castle from wishes and pies,
With jellybean windows and chocolate skies.
The neighbors came with their own sweet plans,
Trading gumdrops and silly cans.

A rainbow bridge connects our hearts,
Gathering stories from all the parts.
While giggling fairies sprout from the ground,
Tickle our souls with laughter profound.

With lanterns made from curious thoughts,
We sailed on ships made of tangled knots.
Adventure awaits just beyond the bend,
Where dreams are comics without an end.

So follow the whims, let joy take the lead,
In this playful journey, we all succeed.
With smiles like sunshine, we'll float on a breeze,
Spreading warmth and laughter with effortless ease.

When Stars Align with Intent

Under cosmic circus tents,
I juggle dreams and events.
With a wink and nod to fate,
I dance on paths, never late.

Twirling thoughts like cotton candy,
Life's flavors sweet, never dandy.
I trip on hopes, take a dive,
But laugh it off, I'm still alive.

Planets roll their eyes at me,
Spinning tales of pure debris.
Stars chuckle through their bright glare,
Guess there's humor in despair.

So I sip my stardust tea,
With a twist of irony.
If you're lost, just grab a map,
It's in the jokes; take a lap.

In the Cradle of Lost Aspirations

In a cradle made of dreams,
I snooze while life cracks at the seams.
With ambitions tucked away tight,
I giggle at my comical plight.

Balloons float past my sleepy face,
Each one holds my forgotten grace.
I chase them with a laugh and grin,
Who knew failures could be a win?

These aspirations, a playful bunch,
Swirl like cereal in a punch.
In the kitchen of my regrets,
Spoons of laughter, no regrets.

So here's to all those wishes grand,
That slipped right through my careless hand.
In this cradle, I find delight,
A humorous twist, a curious flight.

Reflections on a Gossamer Path

On threads of silk, I tiptoe soft,
Where thoughts glide up and dreams aloft.
Mirrors giggle, wise and sly,
As I question all, oh my!

Waves of doubt, they tickle toes,
In this maze where nonsense flows.
Do I take the left or right?
Flip a coin, it's all alright!

Gossamer strands, a breath away,
Whisper secrets of the day.
With each turn, a jest unseen,
Life's a riddle wrapped in green.

So dance along this whimsical trail,
With every misstep, I prevail.
Through reflections, sunlight gleams,
Finding laughter in my dreams.

The Alchemy of Being Alive

In the lab of existence bright,
I mix wonders, oh what a sight!
Bubbling thoughts and giggles, too,
Creating potions just for you.

Experimenting with my fate,
I cast a spell, can't hesitate.
With beakers full of silly cheer,
Transmuting doubts, I persevere.

The recipe asks for a dash,
Of laughter stirred with a splash.
I let the chaos swirl and dance,
In this alchemy, I find romance.

So raise a glass to life's sweet brew,
With all its flavors, old and new.
In this potion, I truly thrive,
Finding magic, being alive.

Seasons of Uncertainty

Spring's here, but I lost my shoes,
Winter's chill makes me choose,
Should I plant or just recline?
Guess I'll flip a coin this time.

Summer sun with no sunscreen,
Burned my nose, now I'm a meme,
Fall brings sweaters, pumpkin spice,
Where's the handbook? That'd be nice.

Dancing leaves fall, calling me,
Chasing squirrels like I'm three,
Should I worry, should I play?
Life's a game gone astray.

Yet here I am, lost in glee,
Life's a riddle, can't you see?
With each season, laugh I must,
In this chaos, there's a trust.

Unwritten Destinies

I woke up today, what to wear?
My closet trembles, knows my despair,
Will I succeed or miss the bus?
All depends on how I fuss.

Lunchbox hero in a suit,
Took my career from corporate loot,
Wrote plans in crayon, oh what fun,
Who needs rules when you're on the run?

Maps are useless when you roam,
Destination? Just call it home,
Each twist and turn a new delight,
Write your story? Nah, I might!

So here's a toast to random tries,
With pizza slices and silly pies,
In unwritten paths, we'll take a chance,
Life's a quirky, silly dance.

Searching for Whispers in the Wind

The breeze keeps laughing, it won't share,
Secrets tangle in my hair,
"Is life a game?" I shout with glee,
"Or just a show on daytime TV?"

Clouds are gossiping, making bets,
While squirrels plot their internet threats,
I seek answers in leaves and skies,
But just find more reasons to improvise.

Grass tickles toes, the trees just shrug,
Wind whispers silly jokes, I hug,
Looking for wisdom like a treasure map,
But all I find is a friendly clap.

So if you see me, lost in thought,
Blame the wind for all I've sought,
In this comedy, I play my part,
Searching for whispers, and a laugh to start.

Echoes of Forgotten Dreams

Last night's goals faded like smoke,
Chasing visions of a stroke of luck,
"Be a star," I shouted loud,
But ended up lost in a crowded cloud.

Once a rockstar, now I'm a joke,
My audience? Just a really curious oak,
Woodpecker critiquing my latest ballad,
Who knew trees had taste so salad?

Ghosts of plans float in the night,
Whispers of "Maybe" and "Alright,"
Yet I smile and raise a toast,
To dreams forgotten, they love me most.

So let's dance to the rhythm of whim,
In this echo chamber, let's not go dim,
For in comedy's arms, we find our scheme,
A laugh is all we need, it seems.

Navigating the Labyrinth of Being

In a maze of thoughts, I stroll,
Sipping confusion from a bowl.
Life's quirks, like socks that disappear,
Laughing at fate, oh dear, oh dear.

Maps are useless, I must confess,
With every turn, I digress.
But isn't that the fun we seek?
Finding joy in every cheeky peak?

Chasing answers, I slip and slide,
On banana peels of cosmic pride.
Life's a jester, always in jest,
Who knew chaos could be such a fest?

So I dance through this tangled plot,
With giggles and snacks, I'm never caught.
In this labyrinth, the only route,
Is to laugh and munch, without a doubt.

Where Joy Meets Sorrow

In a teacup of mirth, I pour,
A splash of sadness at the core.
Tickling frowns for a hearty laugh,
In this silly, sappy photograph.

Juggling woes like circus clowns,
Looking for smiles in frown-filled towns.
A twinge of sorrow, a hearty cheer,
Comedic relief is always near.

Life's a sitcom, in twisted scenes,
Where laughter bursts at the seams.
I tiptoe on both sides of the tide,
Balancing joy with a teary-eyed slide.

So when gloom knocks, I just wave,
With a punchline ready, mischief I crave.
In this dance of spots and stripes,
I find humor in what life types.

Finding Solace in the Chaos

Amidst the chaos, I'm all a-chuckle,
Sorting my thoughts in a jumbled huddle.
Entropy wraps me in a warm hug,
Like a giant, grinning, fuzzy bug.

Lost in a world of tangled threads,
I look for wisdom where the sidewalk spreads.
With every step, I slip and trip,
But hey, that's just the cosmic whip!

A sandwich here, a donut there,
Finding refuge in sugary despair.
I laugh with noodles wrapped 'round my head,
Hey, who knew wisdom wasn't all bread?

So here's to chaos, clumsy and bright,
Where the wrongs feel so dazzlingly right.
In this circus, I take my stance,
With jellybeans in the foolish dance.

A Soul's Journey Through Eternity

With a packed bag and a wobbly shoe,
On this endless trip, what's a soul to do?
Floating through ages, I trip and twirl,
In this timeless dance, around I swirl.

Each lifetime's a game of hopscotch divine,
Where laughter echoes as the stars align.
Dodging moments like dodgeball pros,
Collecting punchlines as the current flows.

In the cosmic theater, all eyes on me,
I juggle my quirks, a fool's jubilee.
There's wisdom in giggles, a message so loud,
Life's stage is for jesters, I'll wear that shroud.

So bring on the ages, bring on the jest,
In this silly journey, I'm truly blessed.
For who needs a map when laughter's the guide?
I'll sashay through forever, with joy as my ride.

Embracing the Unknown

Life's a puzzle with some pieces missing,
We dance in circles, hoping, not hissing.
A world of wonders, odd and kooky,
Clumsy explorers, feeling quite spooky.

With every wrong turn, I learn to embrace,
A jumbled existence, a wild goose chase.
Tickling my fancy, life's curious quirks,
I'd rather be lost than follow the perks.

Searching for Stardust

In the attic of dreams, I rummage around,
Finding old treasures, not lost but profound.
A sprinkle of stardust, a pinch of delight,
Tickling my toes in a cosmic moonlight.

Chasing the sparkles, where do they go?
The universe giggles, it's all just for show.
With laughter in my pocket, I leap and I whirl,
As stardust keeps falling, giving life a twirl.

Where Dreams Take Root

Beneath the surface, ideas take flight,
Planting small wishes by day and by night.
With giggles and grins, they blossom and grow,
In a garden of dreams, there's plenty to sow.

Scarecrows of worries stand tall and absurd,
Guarding the laughter that creeps without word.
Where hope finds a haven, and folly's in bloom,
I dance with my shadows, and sweep all the gloom.

Paradoxes of Time

Tick-tock goes the clock, or does it rewind?
I sip on my coffee, but I'm unconfined.
Moments are squishy, they stretch and they bend,
Like rubber band memories that never quite end.

I trip on my future while gazing ahead,
Caught in a whirlwind, it spins 'til I'm dead.
Laughing at minutes that run in a loop,
Life's little circus, I'm just part of the troupe.

Every Path Leads Home

I wandered down a road of socks,
With mismatched shoes and ticking clocks.
A GPS that spun in glee,
Said, "Turn around, you'll find the key."

I tripped on laughter, fell on dreams,
Collected thoughts like wayward beams.
Each twist and turn, a playful jest,
Leading me to my silly quest.

My compass pointed to dessert,
Skidding past the sage of hurt.
What's home, if not a cozy chair?
With snacks and friends and lighthearted air.

So here I sit, with crumbs galore,
The search for meaning? What a chore!
As every path loops back with style,
I'll just enjoy it, mile by mile.

In Search of Invisible Keys

I searched for keys in fluffy clouds,
With hopes to join the dreaming crowds.
They told me first, to clear my mind,
Yet all I found was mismatched kind.

A garden full of tangled vines,
And squirrels that danced in jester lines.
An endless quest for locks obscure,
Where laughter seemed the only cure.

The keys I sought were hid in puns,
In silly jokes and wobbly runs.
They're not in boxes, nor in drawers,
Just giggles shared and open doors.

So if you lose your keys at night,
Just wink at stars; they'll shine so bright.
For life's a jape we help design,
And in the laughter, we align.

Tides of Thought

The waves of thought, they come and go,
Like jellybeans in a flowy show.
I surf on whims and ride the breeze,
While seagulls giggle at my unease.

A shoreline built of chalk and charm,
Where silly fish just wish to disarm.
Each tide brings secrets, fresh and bold,
And stories of the ones who're old.

With every splash, I ponder deep,
While crabs below just hide and peep.
The meaning sinks like ships in foam,
Yet makes me feel that I am home.

So when you dip your toes in life,
Let laughter be your guiding knife.
For in the swell, you'll surely find,
The joy that wraps around your mind.

Where Time Stands Still

In a land where clocks forgot to tick,
I found a chair that made me sick.
It squeaked and creaked with every thought,
But to this pause, my heart was caught.

With sandwiches that laughed and cheered,
And kettle corn that always appeared.
No rush, no fuss, just blissful stay,
Where time was busy, lost in play.

I counted jellybeans on the floor,
Each one, a thought I could explore.
In stillness, I found dance inside,
With every giggle as my guide.

So if you hear the clocks protest,
Just settle in and take a rest.
For in this place of silent glee,
You'll find the fun of just being free.

The Unwritten Chapters of Me

I wandered through the shelves of time,
In search of answers like a rhyme.
Each page a pun, each line a jest,
Who knew my life was a sitcom quest?

The coffee spills, the socks misplaced,
In life's great book, I'm underdressed.
I write my tales in mismatched pens,
And laugh at my own plot's loose ends.

With gumdrops stuck in golden hair,
I skip through lands of wild despair.
A clown in search of cosmic sense,
I juggle thoughts from hence to thence.

So here's my tale, all weird and spry,
With happy flops and wild old ties.
In chapters blank, I'll likely find,
A laugh or two, and peace of mind.

A Map of Stars and Stories

In the sky's vast book, I took a peek,
Found stars that winked and some that squeaked.
Their stories flared in cosmic fun,
Like jokes that fly just before they run.

A comet passed with a cheeky grin,
It said, "Join us on a dizzy spin!"
I danced along the Milky way,
With space candy clouds on a bright buffet.

Would you believe I tripped on Mars?
Got tangled up in Venus' bars.
I rode the rings of Saturn's dress,
And left some giggles in the mess.

So now I chart my quest for laughs,
In cosmos wide, with quirky paths.
Each star a giggle, each planet a pun,
In this rolled scroll, the trip's the fun!

Dancing with the Abyss

I tangoed with the void one night,
His shoes were clumsy, but what a sight!
He stepped on dreams and twirled my fears,
And laughed while I just shed warm tears.

We swayed through shadows, all askew,
His cold embrace surprisingly grew.
I wore bright socks, he wore a frown,
As we twirled 'round the cosmic town.

I whispered jokes, he took a pause,
And wobbled back, defying laws.
Flipped my worries to silly flips,
As we danced through space on cosmic trips.

When dawn broke in a wacky spree,
He vanished, but left a laugh with me.
In the depths, I found a silly grace,
Dancing on jokes in the abyss's space.

Dust and Stardust

In a cupboard full of dust and dreams,
I found a box of pause and beams.
With every puff, the memories flew,
Of wild delights and laughs anew.

The grandma ghosts made cookies tall,
While dust bunnies joined for an impromptu ball.
They'd laugh and share their ghostly cheer,
In dancing shoes, it's all so clear!

There's magic lurking in dirty nooks,
With dusty tales and funky hooks.
A sprinkle here, a giggle there,
The universe loves a funny affair.

So next time dust claims a corner tight,
Remember, joy hides in plain sight.
In stardust dreams and giggly mess,
There's meaning here, I must confess!

Raindrops on a Wandering Mind

Raindrops dance on my window sill,
Pondering jokes, I sit and chill.
Did I leave my keys under the bed?
Or was that my lunch, now full of dread?

Clouds roam freely, my thoughts do too,
Searching for wisdom in a pickle stew.
Do socks have feelings when they're alone?
Or is that just me, in this brainy drone?

When life gives lemons, make a face,
Then squeeze them right back into space.
I tripped on a thought, fell flat on my goal,
Yet laughter still bubbles, like soda on a roll!

So here I linger, pudding in hand,
Trying to grasp what I might have planned.
The joy is in tangents, not easy or neat,
Dancing in circles, oh how sweet!

The Hues of Hesitation

In a sea of choices, I take a pause,
Do I want sushi or just a hot cause?
Life's palette shifts from bright to dull,
I paint with my fears, while I munch on a mull.

Flavors of fear are a spicy delight,
Sipping on doubts under the moonlight.
Twirling between colors, a dizzying whirl,
Does fate know my plans, or just laugh and twirl?

Should I rock the boat or shore up the seams?
Juggling my dreams like they're ice cream beams.
The clock ticks on, while I sip on my tea,
Do I want to dive in, or just want to flee?

Am I a painter or just a clown?
With brushstrokes of giggles in a quirky town.
Each choice a ripple, lifting a cheer,
Oh, hue me happy, and let's shift gear!

Between Yesterday and Tomorrow

Caught in a loop, like a hamster's race,
Yesterday waved, 'Take it at your pace!'
Tomorrow chuckled, 'You might want to run,'
But I just created a mess with my fun.

The clock's a magician, pulling hairs,
Who knew time's humor was filled with layers?
Yesterday's regrets, a parade of clowns,
Tomorrow's just waiting for me to fall down.

In the middle I stutter, between laughs and tears,
Trying to balance my hopes and my fears.
Do I chase a rainbow or nap on a breeze?
Maybe just binge-watch silly cat-MCs?

A moment's a gift wrapped in joy and jest,
Smiling at life, I give it my best.
Between yesterdays laughs and future's surprise,
I sip on the laughter, and let out a sigh.

In Pursuit of the Unseen

I'm off on a quest for the missing sock,
Who knew such treasure could rock my block?
With coffee in hand, I embark on this spree,
The world's full of wonders, just wait and see!

In the realm of lost things, the absurd runs wild,
Do spoons dream of sugar, in kitchens compiled?
My thoughts are like kittens, they tumble and play,
Swimming through chaos, in a curious way.

I tripped over wisdom, fell flat on my nose,
The hidden truths hide beneath all my clothes.
But I laugh with the shadows, they whisper and tease,
Life's full of nonsense, a baffling breeze!

So onward I wander, giggling along,
In pursuit of the unseen, where I belong.
With a wink and a jig, I chase what I deem,
Life's quirky adventures, a whimsical dream!

The Colors of Belonging

In a world where socks go missing,
Colors blend, quite dismissing.
Purple laughs with shades of green,
Orange winks, a playful scene.

In this jumbled hue parade,
Friendship's spark, never delayed.
Crazy patterns, all askew,
A kaleidoscope, just for you.

Life's a canvas, splattered bold,
Tales of laughter, sweetly told.
Step inside this quirky frame,
Colors dance, without a shame.

Though some may take it too to heart,
We paint our lives, a work of art.
And if at times we're feeling blue,
Just add some yellow, mix it through.

Echoes of a Silent Heart

Whispers float on a breezy night,
Bouncing back with such delight.
A timid heart beats soft and low,
Yet in this hush, a laugh can grow.

Questions dwell in silent rows,
Like socks tangled up in throes.
Yet laughter breaks the quiet's reign,
Echoing sweet like a summer rain.

With every sigh and giggling sigh,
We share the tales that zoom and fly.
In moments caught where silence drapes,
A shout of joy, the heart escapes.

So, let them whisper, let them tease,
Our quiet souls, they chuckle with ease.
In echoes, warmth begins to swell,
Yes, even silence can be quite the sell.

The Weight of Unasked Questions

Questions hang like laundry lines,
Heavy washing, tangled finds.
What's the secret to a good pie?
Why do socks vanish? Oh, my!

The wonders live in just the air,
Like missing keys or a cat's stare.
Why's the sky so blue, they say,
Yet answers playfully run away?

With laughter echoing in my head,
I ask my plants, they laugh instead.
For all that's lost, a puzzle piece,
Let's dance around, find our release.

So hold those questions, give a wink,
Life's a riddle, let us think.
And if the weight feels just too much,
Just laugh a little; life's soft touch.

A Symphony of Moments

Each tick of time, a clap of hands,
Moments dance like rubber bands.
From silly pranks to stumbles sweet,
Life's a tune, a rhythmic beat.

With every chuckle, every sigh,
Life's an orchestra, oh my, oh my!
A trumpet's blast, a drum's soft thump,
Join in the fun, give life a jump.

We play our parts, both high and low,
In this concert, we steal the show.
With friends who harmonize the best,
In this life, we're truly blessed.

So let the music swirl and rise,
A symphony beneath the skies.
Together we'll dance, no fear nor fret,
In each note of laughter, there's joy yet.

www.ingramcontent.com/pod-product-compliance
Lightning Source LLC
Chambersburg PA
CBHW071845160426
43209CB00003B/428